THE COLLECTED POEMS
OF DIANA MANN
(A journey through her life)

Any proceeds raised from this publication will be donated
to Diana's favourite charities -
Brooke Hospital for sick animals, The Donkey Sanctuary,
Jerry Green Foundation, Animal Health Trust & RSPCA-North Essex branch.

First published in 2006 by
Michael Mann
The Chantry, Church End,
Stebbing, Dunmow,
Essex CM6 3SW

Printed in Great Britain by
Moffat Press Group, London
Tel: 020 8548 2966

Diana with her beloved dogs, Suzie & Finn

Diana

Diana's early life was troubled, (and that must be the largest of understatements). Having run away from every school she was sent to, she finally achieved her ambition and was enrolled in the Guildhall School of Dramatic Art. She graduated with distinction and went straight onto the London stage.

However, within weeks, the outbreak of war put an end to that. She did service in the Red Cross through the London blitz and subsequently joined the Air Transport Auxiliary (in a ground staff capacity). Then she joined the W.R.N.S, where I met her in 1942. She was undoubtedly the best visual signaller I encountered in my service.

We married in 1945 and settled, when both demobilised, in the islands in the West of Scotland. When my job there collapsed, I returned to schoolmastering and by 1949 we settled in Stebbing, where we lived until her death on January 27th 2005.

Of Diana's two passions, one was her garden, the other was poetry. She had had one or two short stories published early on but poetry soon became her all consuming passion. She joined the Essex Poetry Society and in due course became, successively, treasurer, secretary, chairman and president until her death.

She was always indifferent to publication of her work, despite my entreaties. I feel I owe it to her memory. I shall say, at this juncture, that she was urged on by Pauline Stainer who, although much younger than Diana, is one of the country's leading poets. Diana's thanks can be seen in 'A gift of poems.'

It will become evident that she was a tireless craftsman. I have divided her work, for the purposes of this book, into several sections.

Poems about her youth, a time of spiritual
loneliness, which included a murder,
of which she was an aural witness.
Poems related to her beloved Cornwall, where
she spent much of her childhood with
her much loved aunt , Ione, and
thereafter, in the same house, with me.
Poems about her home in Stebbing, equally
loved, and its surroundings.
General poems, which have no territorial
or family connection.
Poems of her short time in Scotland and
her visits to Spain.

I hope you enjoy them. They are a constant solace to me, now that she is no longer with us and it is my hope that they will touch you, too.

My warmest thanks go to Pauline Stainer, poet of great distinction and an old and valued friend of Diana and me, for agreeing enthusiastically to write the foreword to this book.

Lastly, I want to record my sincere and heartfelt thanks to my neighbours, Sharon & Geoff Bareham. Sharon who looked after Diana so devotedly in her last illness, has fair copy typed the entire text meticulously. Geoff has taken it from her and designed and published the book you now hold. Without their devoted efforts and technical expertise, it would never have seen the light of day.

Michael Mann

FOREWORD
By Pauline Stainer

In praise of Diana Mann

I knew Diana for many years, as a close friend and as a poet. She was intensely private about her writing and never sought publication. But she wrote in the tradition of John Clare and Edward Thomas, with a naturalist's eye, clear and vivid, like Gilbert White's. Her physical beauty was reflected in the 'candour' of her style. (And I use the word in its original sense of 'purity'). She weighed every word scrupulously, and having trained as an actress had an excellent ear for the musicality of language. She told me how sometimes she scribbled late into the small hours in her tiny writing-room, with its patchwork quilt, on the very edge of Stebbing grave-yard.

Her poems reveal a love of landscape, and of that perfect blend of wilderness and discipline which made her garden so magical. She knew too, like St Francis, what creatureliness was - and found herself waylaid by donkeys and goats peering through Cornish hedges, bringing them food she should have eaten herself.

She retained to the end, a girlish quality, a child's eye glimpse of the first-timeness of the world. Hers was a rare spirit. No wonder the wild birds fed from her hand.

CONTENTS

DEDICATED POEMS

A gift of poems
(for Pauline Stainer)

Angels
(for Iona Opie)

Travelling Tradescant
(for Michael Hynds)

A GIFT OF POEMS

Now I have leave to enter
the place that you inhabit,
the blue-white clinical room
with its range of cold
meticulous instruments
bladed and pointed
for immaculate dissections.

Which, in dream-like
synchronicity,
is also alchemist's cell
where trees root in the floor
and blood under the microscope
is the dark blood of the ballads.
Where the stone repugns probing.

I see you poised
perilously between mind-light
and earth-pull, grasping
a hawk's winged equilibrium
in the pinioned image -
with calculation of words
the stoop's taut precision.

Each poem a balancing act.

ANGELS

Beneath medallioned rafters
They hang on windhover wings,
Ringleted, helmeted,
Their girlish inscrutable faces
Wan from a long watch.

Angels, but soldierly,
Their garb and their emblems
And that attent stiff stance
The schema of crusaders.
These corpse-like spirits
Jar into focus
The once-holiness of war.

And gently, as an aside
The scarring of rent lovers.
Angels identically paired
They fly two amplitudes,
Due west through mists of unknowing,
Eastwards on course for the Host.

They are beetled by metal,
Each like a high bird pinked
By rains of round-headed shot.
Hazed light from clerestory windows.

TRAVELLING TRADESCANT

So he's flying out of winter,
the gardens he tends lovingly
left fallow, out of his hands.

Best time to go, the year's first month
forging iron in the earth, spade
shining clean in the shed.

He'll fly with the sound of music
capped in his ears, will doze
the celestial journey South.

Tuned in to Madrigals.
He's saved all year for this
bonanza of being himself,

Sun-worshipper at large
in a land of unwinking sun,
Musician Extraordinary

At courts of those emigrants
avid for cadences
belonging them to home.

He'll return to bird's plain song,
primroses and catkins. Glad to be here
and restless to be gone.

POEMS ABOUT HER YOUTH

Yew Place

The Lesson

Continuum

The Masque

YEW PLACE

My father would go there
after dinner, summer evenings.
I'd watch from the window
chilly in my nightgown
tracing him into the dark
invisibility of trees.

He never came back.
I was asleep by then.
He must have touched midnight
in that gappy jointed circle
of yews like standing stones
intentional and sacred

as relics of lost myth.
I'd think of him there
cross-knee'd on the wood seat
in the blackening shadows,
the star-lit wet grasses
winking one emerald.

He was lonely and hard
as a thin-skinned crab,
too sour for milk tooth tasting.
But I slept easier
for knowing he sought
the enfolding of darks

Where we could meet.
Our tryst was never spoken.

THE LESSON

At dinner you would give me
an inch of rufous wine,

pouring ceremoniously
to teach me reverence
for transient rarity.

It swam in the tilted glass
like a genie liquified,
magically spiritous,
fumey with cellar'd musts.
But on those August evenings

the things I noticed most
were the tree outside the window
hung heavy with red apples;
its shadow on the grass,
and your white skin-flint knuckles

as you poured, saying "drink".
I thought these were eternal
because they preceded my time,
because they set a pattern
that appeared immutable.

Now they parcel the past
into distinct bright images
fleetingly recurrent.
Samuel Palmer's tree, long felled
on its shadow, is framed to last
just so long as I remember.

Your pouring hand is ash.
But still the indelibly rare
is linked with transience;
as when a sun-dawn mists
whitely these solemn trees

or a hand reaches a hand
to interlock ten fingers.
The instant recognised
is stored like good wine.
Your lesson was seminal.

CONTINUUM

I was ten when the beech was felled
for safety after a gale.
It left a blank like death

It could be your death, on a smaller scale,
but the shock of each loss has made
the same hole in the sky,

A hole for habitation.
Learning to live in a gap needs time.
Only habit, that weed of days

Fills, at length, the hollow
left by a familiar.
After you died I planted

Foxgloves, wild arum, cowslips
to make a wilderness
not thinking at the time

that I delved a wasteland
to pump out pain through fingers
ligatured to earth.

When I was ten I planted rue,
a slip from the old bush
which smelled strongly of nothing else

Knowing even then an end
is a beginning if a root will strike,
leaves fecundate a silence.

THE MASQUE

The most I remember, for I was a child wing-clipped
To a small high room in the long-locked hours of sleep time,
Is the black and the white of the moon hung high in a tree,
And a silvered lawn, dark yews, the light of water.
People were there, but not with their daytime faces,
People as black and white as the yews and the moon,
Quick-silvering over the grass and under the cedars,
Urgent as rooks disturbed in a wood at nightfall.

'A masque', my nursemaid had told me, 'that's what's to be,
And don't let me catch you catching your death at the window.
It's not for children', she said. So of course I waited
And slipped out of bed as the stable clock struck midnight.
How long the masque had been going, how long I'd slept
I could not say; I imagined those winging figures
Were acting, and the scream that had jerked me awake
Belonged in the play. It was long-drawn-out, like an owls',
A terrible throbbing wail. And then it silenced,
And a hum, like a swarm of bees, rose up to my window.
I must have slept. In the morning the house was different.
Something had happened. The servants talked in whispers;
And the faces were grave. I wondered why everything changed,
And why, soon, the house was shut, and we went away.
'Did they scream in the masque?' I kept asking.
But nobody answered. I garnered some garbled words
About death, and a lady. It happened so long ago.
Now you come asking. Did you say 'documentary?'
'A princess of Russia?' I know nothing at all about her.
I remember the moon in a tree, the wail of an owl.
Forgive me, the masque has slipped from my recollection.

GENERAL POEMS

A BOOK FOR YOUNG NATURALISTS
(GIVEN TO ROSE LLOYD ON HER BIRTHDAY, APRIL 24TH 1854)

(The first poem Diana ever wrote)

This book speaks from an age grown gravely young;
Breathes cowslips innocence; its light. prim sentences
Sound morning-minted as a thrush's song.

Did Rose Lloyd pluck its riches? She whose name
Rambles the cover. If so, her careful fingers
Garnered for her a demure posthumous fame,

No greater than a gravestone would afford,
But sweeter. All we may know of her
Is here, her life concentred to a word,

Her small world shrunk to what these pages tell
Of fern and flower, its mood elusive as a thought
That gropes to seal an image to a smell

Of apples, hay or woodsmoke. Her gift is now my book.
I try to read it through her unstained eyes,
And learn, as she must once have done, to look.

SENTRY

There's a bonfire on the verge,
a grey circle of ash
fringing the blackened char
and dull crimson rash

of spent flame. One live ember
crouched in the fire's core
glows to the touch of a gust
and its blown bright spore

seizes on tussock and leaf.
There's an instant flare
then dark crowds thickly in
to stab you aware

of how it chills to remain
far out on night's cleft
hearing voices dwindle away
and being the one who's left

with night to shoulder alone
counting stars like sheep
through the slow drag of small hours
to ward off sleep.

FALCON

Home from the Game Fair
remember the grip of the falcon
poised on a gauntleted fist
belled, hooded, alert.

Tiercel unsure of his feet
he rides the lifted wrist
precipitously
as an acrobat on a wire
teetering for balance.

Then stands rock-still
pinned to the starting post
all muscle to be off.

Bullets into the blue
accommodating air,
a shooting star ascending
to the black speck of himself
hung cruciform to windward,
a mote in the sun's blinding.

He will elude observation
and falconer's entreaty
until he has slaked his need
to feel spread wings free-wheeling
up heady lifts of thermals;

Until his ballistic eyes
have hurtled their fill of fear
to the pricked nerves of his quarry
and sprung tension releases
the lightning bolt of the stoop.

At length deigns to perform
display of aerobatics
arrowing in wing-pinioned
to swoop, bank and flash
with faultless aim the arena,
skimming the skipping-rope lure
which he takes after teasing with misses.

His hearing drums with applause.
He tears the meagre flesh
from a rabbit's foot
then mounts the qauntlet
in the heat and disdain of his pride.

QUESTIONS

Where's foxy? the child asked
has foxy gone away?
I watched him every morning
at the break of day.

He'd run past the woodshed
and sit up on the lawn
to scratch his back like Collie-dog
and stretch a snarly yawn.

I liked the way his brush swept
his footpath from behind.
Its bristles were a soft as fur
and bright as orange rind.

Shut that trap his Dad said,
polishing a gun.
If y'er soft on foxes
y'er no a farmer's son.

The boy asked his mother
is our foxy dead?
You and I are one, dear,
was all his mother said.

GNATS

The air is their ballroom.
They dance in the roseate glow
Of sun-smoke under the trees.

Their dance is a sarabande,
Slow stepless weaving of bodies
In trance, that do not touch.

There are no partners.
On the vertical floor
Myriads evolve a stately measure.

Procession without progress,
Motion steeped in stillness,
Change held over constant

Are their means to no evident end
Save this starry celebration
Of evanescence, dying light.

POWER CUT

Candle, my companion,
You watch me washing shirts,
Moving light while I move soapy water,
We two, accomplishing.
How is it you endow with dignity
What the bright bulb shrinks to drudgery?
How do you give the commonplace
A grace, a timeless quality?

You are no slave-driver
Goading me on with a glare,
No marvel of technology
Exacting tributes to efficiency.
You are serene and humble.
You shed your mystery
Gently on hand and task,
Your eye on my eye's level,
Your nimbus gravely wavering,
And your small stature lessening
The while you add to mine.

BABY SITTING

I am left this child.
They didn't dump her exactly
but their car snorted impatience
as they briefed me at the door.

'If she cries don't worry.
Here's the phone number.
Promise we won't be late.'

I enfold her into the hall.
We two, both warily alone
in a stranger's dark encounter.
I examine her closely
by the waver of candle-flame.
Her eyes blink messages
of minuscule alarm
lips pucker and work
at absent teats. Her hands
clench then slowly unscroll like fronds.

There should be between us
some kind of mute rapport,
surely some recognition
of mutual helplessness?
I finger the pale fluff
furring her naked scalp.
She grows still as a bird does
when you stroke its head.

The dreaded wail is quite soft,
forlorn, an animal cry
of helpless abandonment.
It is the cry
of lovers wrenched one from the other,
of a whole world divided -
her discovery of bereavement.
It is too soon. Too soon
to be one who is left.
She is learning treason.

Now she's gone suddenly quiet,
munches air, blinks
flame-dazzle out of her eyes.
I touch her hand, her fingers
tendril my finger,
they're prehensile as ivy,
as the tail of a monkey.
Such strength!

She may be stronger than I am,
a little bundle of life force
packed with kicks and hollers.
She does not look for response,
only for obedience,
does not question her rights
but assumes them like a queen
deposed, demanding restitution.

And now like a daisy closing
at the onset of nightfall
she curls, quite suddenly,
into the armour of sleep.

I hold her growing weight
in the crook of my arm.
She weighs nine pounds of potatoes
or a bucketful of seaweed.
The candle gutters out.
We're still in the dark, we two,
but sharing each other, sharing.

BOUGHT FLOWERS

We buy them for a party.
They look funereal.
White lilies like ivory
carved into pre-Raphaelite shapes;
pallid carnations; double freesias
immaculately scentless.

They are the ornament
of a disordered room,
the chairs set back,
rugs rolled and put away,
prized objects shoved out of sight.

They will reign for three hours
totally disregarded
while cacophony of talk
wells to a crescendo,
glasses are drained and replenished.

Tomorrow, the compost heap.
And for the single friend
we'll gather our simple flowers,
cow parsley, white rocket,
rose campion, feverfew
for a jug on the kitchen table.

WITHOUT AVAIL

They hang from the rafters in bunches.
Dried flowers. A rope of onions. Herbs.
She never takes them down. They gather dust.
They are what she planned her life was going to be.

Craftsmanlike. Countrified. Busy with making, with
sowing and reaping. Still she wears the dress
as brown as earth that was to be her habit.
But somehow the part didn't fit.

Now, desolate among fag-ends, magazines,
she wonders what became of her vocation,
Has discovered one simple fact -
It takes two to enter this discipline.

OLD FRIENDS

Such mean small rain, each drop of clinging wet
squeezed from a miser sky. Beneath a shared umbrella
there may be closeness, or a different state.
Not enmity or coolness, merely the queer hollow
sense of not meeting. Goodwill on both sides.
Attempts to please. Knock-up of casual talk
disclaiming by its tone what it confides
of shared remembering. We know each other's walk
and keep in step; we know each other well enough to know
how our tongues side-step, shying from rapport.
It seems important to remain just so,
detached and friendly, giving vague support
throughout the widening yawn of afternoon
though loneliness descends diffuse as rain.
This is the vacuum where love should have been.
For God's sake fill it till you catch your train.

AUNT ELAINE

After a stiff, snubbed childhood, Aunt Elaine
Attained to English rosehood, exhaustively recorded
In sepia snapshots; now caught sitting on the grass
Hugging a dachshund and laughing; now leaning on an urn
Pensive in white lace, intent on a flower.
So to the wedding, hand poised above the cake,
Eyes downcast at the enormity of her prospect.
Then instant middle-age. A lifetime of small ailments,
Pet doctors in attendance, husband not,
He being in the city, or on the golf course,
Or at the mysterious Lodge. Aunt Elaine
At home on Wednesday afternoons, and at home
On every afternoon in her empty room,
Knitting, doing crosswords, taking tablets,
And feeling lonesome. Horrible Aunt Elaine
Dutifully visited on Sundays, Dear Aunt Elaine
Visited in widowhood, suddenly nicer
And sad, a staid figure in mourning
Full of Uncle Henry's excellence.
It is rumoured he drank, and the marriage
My dear was never consummated,
Hence, of course, his whisky and her ailments.
Finally, Darling Aunt E. visited joyfully
In her extreme old age, never appearing to mind
The tactless kindness or more hurtful tact
Her vulnerability solicited,
Receiving these, indeed, with gaiety
Spiced with a hint of irony, as homage.
Beloved Aunt E. at last so fully living,
The love pent up through childhood, English rosehood,
Wifehood and widowhood, abundantly outflowing;
Freud had no word for this.

VISITING

Dear Madeleine, I may not come again
(not that you'll notice my absence
and anyway the place is bright and clean,
the staff so kind). It doesn't really make sense
to spend two hours by your bedside. And besides,
the old folk in the lobby stare at the floor
and don't look up. Sounds crazy, but one hides
one's own face too, feeling, well, guilty for
being a visitor, home to go to, and above all free.
They're stuck in their wheel-chairs, having been trundled there
in single file, like jail-birds, from afternoon tea.
(Of course they enjoy every care).

We only clicked once, all this afternoon.
Eyes closed in your grown-smaller face
you mistook me for somebody else and called me June.
'My dear friend June! I'd always know that voice.'
So I was June, till you fitted into a slot
in your fumbling memory, my name
and vaguely remembered, immediately forgot
its context. We had a moment's wavelength all the same.
'Tesekkur ederim,' you said. "That's Turkish and it means
thank you so much. He walked me down the aisle
and I said 'tesekkur ederim' and it means
thank you very much.' My smile met your smile.

Beyond the window, through leafy sycamore trees
big flocks of starlings bustled in and out,
raucously free. Somewhere closer, caged, and there to please
somebody caged in bed, a budgie sang. Such a bright
whistling song. It hurt. Madeleine dear
I think your long captivity of being ill,
brave and confused, is more that I can bear.
So, forgive me if I do not come to call
you Madeleine and reiterate my name
over again. A meeting of lost identities
has nothing to say. I'm not June. You're not the same
merry Madeleine. They're broken, all out ties.
All I could give you is a mistaken presence
holding your hand. But then, today you said
'don't go.' And I said 'I'll be back.' Just once.
Or twice at most. Enough to keep my word.

OLD AGE

The world has changed,
it seems like overnight.
After the upward climb
here am I stumbling down.
The earth gapes open.
I do not look. I am feeling my way
through strange words, foreign attitudes.
They are clotting their faces with hair
like women in a madhouse,
these new inhabitants.
Who are they hiding from?
I am only a sore thumb
bandaged in habit.
I will not hobble you
with my frayed ropes of failure,
snag you with stale complaints.
I know the ultimate answer;
the sun will swell and swallow
this cosmic pill we ride on.
There is no solace for the bald disaster
of being you and me. I have learnt that now.
You hate the lesson branded in my eyes.
My withering dims your stars.

THE ODD ONE OUT

She lived alone
growing each grinding year
more odd and angular
like a thorn tree
screwed into arthritic shapes
by a thin prevailing wind.

They thought her a witch.
Her black cat and magpie
omened ill magic.
Boys pelted her with apples.
Housewives at doorsteps
fell silent as she passed.

She died unmourned,
was given scant burial
north side of the church.
No flowers were placed there.
In time speedwell and daisies
clothed her anonymity.

One Spring a travelling man
came door to door, enquiring
'Anyone seen Ada?
'Gone and good riddance!
Where you come from, then?'
'From everywhere,' he said.

No one recalled him
but in the muggy air
of make-believing hindsight
stories grew like mushrooms.
One knew about a lover,
another how, forsaken,
Ada was taken queer.

'Poor soul.' They blew on pity
fanning such solicitude
as remedied old rancours.
An unrecognisable girl
visited their fantasies,
whose sweet compliant nature
had been early set askew
by derangement of the heart.

So she, quite singular,
born a non-conformist
latterly joined the flock.
Someone raised funds for a headstone.

ESCAPIST

"That was my life", she says above the teacups.
She views it with detachment, as one dead,
Seeing it whole and finished, finding it good perhaps,
Lived out, accomplished, and put by in her head.
She lifts the earned cup to her smiling lips.

I envy her. I have not found a way
Of hanging my life on any acceptable peg.
My rags of moments, feelings, flap and sway.
No Movement galvanises me; the big
Concerns of the committed pass me by.

Only the earth itself, its lights and shapes
Fitfully changing, and the stillness at the core,
May sometimes free me into wide landscapes,
And make of being human something more.
Life seems well lost for these unearned escapes.

GORILLA

His human gesture of lament
Surely means something different;
Pride, perhaps, in apely power,
Or menace, or the stir of lust.
Yet seeing him imprisoned there,
All wild potential gone to rust,
Shambling aimless round and round,
Or seated bored beside his bars,
Who could be sure he does not pound
That mighty chest with fists like ours,
In anguish, or an ape's equivalent?

THE COUNTRY BUS

How like an old, long-married pair
They were, sitting sedate and small
On a front seat, he with an arm
Round her shoulder, holding her there
As if to enclose her from harm;
And neither talking at all.

And when the bus stopped how he guided her
With a stately, old-fashioned care;
She might have been blind, but her eyes
Were alive with delight at the stir
Of the market day crowd. I'd surmise
He was ten, the wiser perhaps by a year.

THE PRISONER

Some winter afternoon in Maida Vale
Or Bayswater - places stuffier then -
The sound of cars on wet roads underlined
A sense of 'there will never come again

A starting point, a freshness, or an hour
Even of ease.' The unearned privilege
Of being young exacted thus its pay.
Seldom such bleak despair beleaguers age.

And now, mid-afternoon beside a fire,
Lapped round with life, and glad of idleness
Fostered by rain, the sound of swishing wheels
Will waken suddenly a vague distress

And throw upon the screen of memory
A room in black and white, aseptic, bare
As station waiting rooms; the ceiling cracks
Traced by a long intent unseeing stare.

No painful incident. No incident.
Merely the room, half-darkness, and the rain;
But somewhere out of sight a prisoner
Begs for release, insistently, in vain,

And if I now protest the bolts are drawn,
He'll counter with 'not when the roads are wet.
Then I am still immured, if momently,
And battened down in darkness I live yet.'

THE LOST CHILDREN

Go. Go quietly, they said.
So the children filed into the wood.
Don't chatter, they said. Keep low.
The children half understood.

The moon rose bald as an eye.
It's cold and it's dark, said a child.
It's not, said another, see here!
A fallen leaf glinted gold.

I want to go home, said a child.
Can't, said another. We're <u>told</u>.
Berries on thorn gleamed robin red
And the barn owl trawled.

Past time for tea, a boy said,
I'm going back for grub.
You stay, said his mate, or you take
a belly-full of drub.

So the children wandered
the bewilderings of the wood
halted by the flick of a fox
then onward, and onward.

The sky in the East glowed red
as a sunset in the west.
That's where I should be, in bed,
a girl said, I'm tired and want to rest.

There's no rest or returning,
a boy said. I know what they knew.
Our homes are burning, burning
there'll be blood in the morning dew.

Look, the moon is bleeding,
the sky is dripping blood.
The children huddled together
like animals in a flood.

SAY IT WITH FLOWERS
LIRA

The flowers you sent me fade.
Red roses wilting on the window sill.
They are like pledges made
Just to be broken. Still
I'll keep them as a token of goodwill

Since once you may have meant
What gifts of roses mean. Now, as they die,
They say our time is spent
Quite clearly, while I try
To write warm thanks. Forgive me for the lie.

A MYTH

Ah unicorn, fleet visitant departing
Without a footfall on snapped twig alerting
Our ears to your swift ripple through the trees -
Without a flicker to amaze our eyes
With your white lissomness - no magic spell
Can ever make you less than mythical
And we must be content though you appear
Too suddenly to make us more aware
Of your fly presence than by catch of breath
Signalling wonder that the quickening myth
Still flashes through the drags of now and here
While we, unfettered by time's barrier
Meet the sprung joy, and in that instant store
A world for which you are the metaphor.

WAYS OF LOOKING

When north winds strip the chestnut tree
And we at last can see
Through latticed branches two brown fields
And sky all summer lost to view,
Then we rejoice that winter yields
So fine a harvest; sky and plough
Together make a landscape grow
Where hitherto a wall of leaves
Rebuffed the eye,
So that we looked for space and light
To small, close things. A drop of dew,
World-shaped and sparkling bright;
A mound of grass
Suggestive of a sheep-cropped hill.
Now, though bare trees allow
The hungry eye to take its fill
We see no further after all;
Close-by, small things extend horizons still.

PROGRESS

No, you can't stop progress, they say,
Meaning, always, you can't stop the rot
Of sprawl and speed, and certainly cannot
Stay the inevitable creep
Towards a dazed hypnotic sleep
Induced by the shrewd parrot cry
That progress is our destiny.
Yet twice-born men
Still quietly say 'be still.
All time is one.
The hub remains the pivot of the wheel.'

YUPPIE ON A TUBE TRAIN

Thousands of voluntary Jonahs disappear into the belly of the
cetacean,
Are forced down into its foetid entrails where rapid peristalsis
takes them,
Half digested, to their exit station.
What does the traveller within the City's guts think, as he hurtles
and rattles along
Winding around arteries of pipes, nerves of cables, and the boney
foundations of office blocks,
Diving deeper than Roman remains, into the clays of forgotten
seas,
Decorated by diatoms, sliding down vertical centuries?
Rising, now, in the midst of an ossuary lapped in lime from
plague days,
Now rustling in the ashes around Pudding Lane, long since
purified in flame,
Do you hear the cries of the chained in the hulks rotting
overhead in the mud of the river,
Or the prayers of prisoners entombed in the Tower or noisome
Newgate?
So many incomplete journeys.
What a satisfaction it is to begin one's ascension at Bank,
Solid symbol of the Everlasting,
Such a comfort to think you have arrived.

POEMS OF
SCOTLAND, CUMBRIA & SPAIN

Landscape poet
St Blanes
The Chieftains

Hill Top, Sawrey

Driving through Spain
Medinaceli

LANDSCAPE POET

Reading of your island birth
Brought it all home;
The bothy facing the sea
Across a field as brown
As the fearless hares of March
That boxed in the sun's limelight;
And the backyard gone to seed
Within its dry-stone walls,
Where wild lupins flaunted
Among wizened gooseberry bushes.
Beyond, a stern grey chapel,
A croft whiter than washing,
And an unimportant foreground
Of cabbage patch and wood pile
Gave skimpy reassurance
That here was grist for living.
Better the crags of Aran,
Blue in the last of sunlight,
Grooved with welts of black shadow,
Uncompromisingly barren.
Ten miles off, or more,
Across a blade of water,
They neighboured the narrow island
Where I dwelt for two lost years,
Unable to force a root
Through soil so alien;
Yet, when at last I left
That landscape, yearning remained,

Hopelessly turncoat,
Sickly with nostalgia
For the place you seeded with words,
To bloom a revelation
Of bleak unconditional beauty.
Now, like you, I go back,
Not in the prodigal flesh,
But in my emigre thoughts,
To find I was native there,
Clamped to that curled sea edge,
Ears intent for curlew,
For packs of greylag casting
Through mist in tumultuous cry:
To find myself still pent there,
Fern-enthralled, entranced by
Scent of fir and fungi,
By the sudden fox that glinted
An instant in a thicket.
But ah, how unresolved
That native stranger remains,
Who, long since a cast-off,
Frets on, hungrily haunting
A time of unfulfillment,
A present never realised,
The past that arrived too soon.

ST BLANES

These are the relics: crumbling dry-stone walls,
A flat slab by the well, the flank of an arch.
But the saint's name is written on these hills
Indelibly. Blane? Blane's? You'd have to search
Back beyond records, burrrow through lost years
To find the Irishman who left his mark
On this land and tongue. One among brothers
But singular. The name lives out his work.
And people follow it, to find the shrine
In these bouldered hills, cast coins in the well.
Sometimes one or two are given a sign.
If pressed, they may talk vaguely of a spell,
Nothing to put a finger on: a scent,
The light - grace incalculably present.

THE CHIEFTAINS

Housed now, propped upright
these tall memorial stones
resurrect the Chieftains
standing at attention
in bascinet, aketon
breeches spurs and poleyns
with hand to spear
shield shoulder-strapped to arm
each body taut and steeled
the man invisible.

If we could see their faces
humanised by fear
fervour or in-
ward glance at her
whose breasts pulse sighs,
eyes rain and parting lips
kiss through a whisper
they would stir to life.

Only the scored beasts.
underwater otter
tailing a swift salmon,
thin-as-a-whip hound
couchant pillowing feet
so comfortably in death
suggest warm hearth and pastime.

Angels and dragons
traced on shield and helmet
are more to the point.
They are the heralds
who establish precedence
record armorial bearings.
They emphasise importance
and how those island lords
needed that pomp and puff
to launch cock-valiant
on course for regions
swallowed in the sky.

HILL TOP, SAWREY
(The home of Beatrix Potter)

We saw the place years back before they made it pay.
There wasn't a car park then, or entrance hut,
And, wonderfully, if you chose your day,
And reached there, say, an hour before they shut
You had it to yourself, a small, mossed house.
The room still kept the scent of daily use,

A blend of burnt wood, lavender and dust
Met at the threshold. At once it made you feel
Half diffident, an uninvited guest
Though not unwelcome. It made the place seem real.
And then, the long case clock that ticked and struck
Softly the hour; a jug of flowers; a book

Open, face upwards on the window seat.
She hadn't left. It was we that were not there.
She moved around, spry, small, not over-neat,
And, plumply settled in the rocking chair,
Ate chocolate, seemed to dream, perhaps of sheep.
We wandered in the meadows of her sleep,

And through a casement saw her meadows turn
Violet at sunset. A glint of lake below
Burned rose, and arching fronds of harts-tongue fern
Caught the light whitely. It was time to go.
She stayed of course. Then, it was still her place,
Still wore the quiet expression of her face.

DRIVING THROUGH SPAIN

Every so often, on the white straight road,
strings of horses, carts laden with dogs and men
joined the stream from the vineyards. Progress is halted
as each fresh influx jostles into place
taking its time to bandy raucous greetings.

Gaining the hill village we're in the throng again,
first-comers still in the saddle, in the square
quaffing, shouting 'holá! Qué tal?'
Men on a high after work. Goatskins jet wine
unerringly from nose-tip into pout
to shouts of 'bien hecho!' It's a simple act
easy as pie, what counts is the bravura.

Driving is disentangling. Down the cobbled hill
emptiness opens like a draught of air.
You slow to avoid three figures walking slowly,
two women and a priest.
Further down a woman runs out of a house
urgently flapping hands, distraughtly urging.

We see through the open top-half of a door
nuns kneeling; four tall lit tapers; lying on a bed
a man or woman like an effigy with folded hands
and pale composed stone face.
Spain, land of contrasts. Joviality and death
so raw and close, such odd confederates.

We drive on through a vacant landscape.
Vineyards, dim moonlight; fifty miles to go.
You say 'we've seen the past. It's nearly over.'
We've never gone back. It's still immediate
and we decided then to keep it so.

MEDINACELI

We came upon it at sunset
a long day's drive from Burgos,
land arid as a slate mine,
The road dry as a wadi.

It jutted up from the plain
with the sharp affront of a rock,
a land-girt jagged island,
rose-red - the incandescence
swarmed in our eyes like blood.

Leafing the summit a green
in a ring of hovels drowsed in shade.
Dilapidated turrets,
an abbey's crenellations
absorbed the heats of sundown.

Morning. A chequered stillness.
Hens scratching for scraps.
One old woman tatting.
Thin voices singing matins.

The tide had long gone out
from this dried bastion
whose duchess had departed
leaving Plateresque ruins
an insignia of grandeur.
Only the low-lolling sun
revived her evening splendour.

Medina of the Sky!
Holy Mother of Christ
benignly smiling on those empty pews.
Piglets rootling a graveyard.
Weeds wedged in a palace wall.
Slow ebb of desuetude.
Here, clear out of the blue
we'd come to earth, reached home.

POEMS OF CORNWALL

Off the Drinnick
Cornish morning
After calling you
Trout fishing
The innocents
Oystercatchers
The Ram
Sycamore
Seal
Waterfall at Hallane
Low tide at Springs, Golant
Stone wilderness
Bodrugan's leap
Heron
Encounter
The snake
Craftsman
Slow worms
For Ione, my aunt

OFF THE DRINNICK

*(For George Bovey, a young farmer who saved the
lives of his neighbour's children at the cost of his own,
off Porth Towan beach, Trenarren)*

Today the sea reveals
perspectives of clean light,
the sun's winking glance
netted under the keel.

Dipped oars trawl ridged sand,
fish-silver quiver
of rocks abruptly wrinkled
by the dive of one finned

Fragment of surface shine.
It was here that he went down,
the sea sparkling its chops
the day blue-gold, the spine

Of the seventh wave
cresting taut as a whale back.
Children were there.
That colossal sieve

Sifted ill from well.
The children, grown, remember
in dreams the saviouring hands,
the long shadow that fell
Like night on their snatched lives.

Knocked cold on a rock
he drifted out just here
back-lashed by muddled waves.

The sea looks so kind,
opens its deeps to the light's
splicing; a smiling grave,
drawn sunblind.

CORNISH MORNING

She sat on the fourth step up, and watched the bees
Nuzzling the fuschia, interminably hopeful.
Drawn to where honey hung, they drove their heads
Deep in the dangling cups, or, practised guests,
Sensed a dead loss and moved on.
But they never left the fuschia, that magnetic
Harvest field of honey in the sun,
And she stayed captive too, cleaved to the letter
The postmen tossed over the wall and into her lap,
A gesture that changed delivery to giving.
Square, white, it twisted down like a leaf,
And she held it unopened, calmly avid as the bees,
Listening to the drone of those small reapers,
Discovering, as they, the taste of honey.

AFTER CALLING YOU

Westward three hundred miles a chosen voice
Echoes numbers I have thought and fingered.
Now airy wires compliant to my choice

Carry my words, their burden, and the light
I am making of this disembodied meeting
Into a room invisibly in sight.

And the easy, casual voice I hear,
Telling of how the trees look, how the sun
Falls on a row of books, speaks in my ear

Of things quite other, the quiet conspiracy
Of being one in millions; of keeping faith
With what we might profess our heresy

Were not that word perhaps too solemn for
So mild a disbelief in certainties.
But oh doubt not the mystery at the core

In view of this unravelling of air,
When, lip to lip across three hundred miles,
You tell me more than words do, and I hear.

TROUT FISHING

He fished, while I, on his camp stool,
Wore out the afternoon. At times
I rose to watch him casting his fly,
Or to enjoy the spectacle
Of nine stock-still fly-wise trout
Nosing the flow in the shallows.

Now and then from the peat-brown depths
Of a far-side pool a lithe fish
Leapt to jack-knife in mid-air
And fall in an arc of silver
To wallop the water; swarms of rings
Eddied outwards, skating the surface.

His line got caught in an alder
Causing agitation of leaves
And a stream of quiet blasphemy.
Then silence. While he twitched his rod
There shot a flash of electric blue
The visible length of the river.

Three kingfishers, or the one returning
Dazzled that stretch while he, intent,
Disentangled his line. Blue bolts
From the blue. I took their indelible
Print on recollection's retina.
He selected a tempting fly.

Then cast in the pool downstream.
In the shade of the bank a dipper,
Dunnock brown, oyster-breasted, bobbed
At the brink like a timid bather,
Soon stepped out dry to a stone, dipped
Small perfunctory curtseys.

I heard the soft plop of his cast,
A gentle reiteration.
Upstream the nine trout still shadowed
The strand, immovably basking.
Above them, two green damselflies
Flashed neon and casually mated,

While by the reed bed, lazily in the currents
Drifted two kinds of weed, one a splayed fan,
The other, fine emerald hair
Sleeked by a brush. Wise travellers,
Their's was an indolent journey,
Onward, onward, stationed against arrival.

He climbed up the steep bank, out of luck.
There followed the usual dismantling,
Packing up. Then, 'no matter,' he said,
'It's been a day on the river.' Well pleased
With his haul of good hours. So, each with our catch,
We sauntered home empty-handed.

THE INNOCENTS

Strolling in single file down to the beach
They looked normal at first. Eight men; but here
Men without women carry fishing rods, and these
Carried no kind of gear.

They smiled, gesticulated rather more
Than most men do, were friendly in a way
Some dogs and children are; one gave the thumbs-up sign
Blithely as who should say

'All's well, and so are we.' Almost he looked
Scholarly with his spectacles, springing hair
Till you noticed his eyes; windows with curtains drawn,
Blanked-out behind the stare.

Beach-happy they picked up stones, threw near and wide,
Slithered on rocks, found shells. As ageing one
Embraced the quiet male nurse who, heedless, watched the sea
Standing as if alone

In thought. Kind, burn-out, how could he respond
To too much love? A prisoner in charge
He seemed to be held there at the pleasure of those
So gleefully at large,

While wheeling high above, gulls free as air
Coasted the currents on white wings outspread.
Innocents too, but strong and simple purposes
Informed each lovely head.

OYSTERCATCHERS

We mean to keep the shoreline to ourselves.
It's where we stand intent with listening eye
for suction-bellied crawling of coiled shells.

We are the instant stabbers. Our quick minds
are sharpened by one purpose. Seek the soft
and succulent interior that winds

slyly out of the carapace. We eat
the living. Are entirely innocent
of lust to kill. Our quarry is salt meat.

We pipe in unison. Our piping keeps
us notified of harvest, signifies
safety in numbers, warns of sudden shapes

stilting over the stones. We understand
minuscule inflections - the rising note
that means 'take wing'. At the shrill command

like a wave we lift, and supple as the sea
head for the reef. We keep ourselves to ourselves.
It is the way that we have elected to be.

THE RAM

That summer evening we clambered to the ram.
Beside the track a stream took the easy way
leaping from rock to rock in its downward climb
over cavernous deeps and shelvings to the sea.

Walks want a reason. There were blackberries
plumper and sweeter than anywhere around
crowding the hut in which the pump's heart beat -
quick rhythmic gulping of water - was the sound
of continuity. We picked blackberries
and stuffed our caps with mushrooms. Took our ease
on the concrete casing of the plunger house
to feel the shock of labour tingle our spines
with its jarring. 'Only one-tenth of the force
of the stream', you said, 'with this engine combines
to water the whole farm'. Incomprehensible,
the steady pulsing trickle of the flow
up through a vein embedded in a hill
as steep as Rough Tor.

We watched a buzzard's slow
wheeling on motionless wings, lifting on thermals
to spin, a speck, in the limitless fading blue.
Everything was ascending, except for the falls
lissomely leaping seawards, but for the level
thud of the pump, old workhorse under the earth,
buried in labour, blackberries for a wreath.

Snatching a grass 'let's go' you brusquely said.
'I feel that ram is counting till I'm dead'.

SYCAMORE

I sit beneath a sycamore
taking its shade like balm
on a burn-wound.

Small areas of sky fidget
between the leaves. Wing buzz
of flies and bees the only sound

until the almost surf-sigh
of leaves twitches my ears.
Tree-talk. Somewhere I read

'The second richest woman
in the world hugs trees.'
Nobody's looking. Shall I hug one too?

The trunk is extremely strong, firm
and consoling. A grey coral
of lichen scabs the bark.

I press against it. Breast,
belly, crotch and thigh. Lichen
gnarls my cheek like a response.

Inside this trunk sap is rising,
as blood is coursing my veins.
It humbles me to realise

both of us are living.

SEAL

Sleek-black as a wet rock
seal basks off-shore
those mild aqueous eyes
appealing dog-like for something.
Could it be company?

As I swim towards him
half watchful, he evades me,
smooth waters fold over
his unperturbed submergence.
I dip my goggled face.

And there he is, alongside,
huge, weighty, lissome,
flippers scarcely moving
as he drifts ahead
and turns and rolls and circles

in a manner which means words
like courteous, humorous, friendly.
I reach out my hand,
it is playfully avoided
within an inch of touching;

contact is eye-to-eye,
and one long gaze suffices.
In the underwater dimness
his nearness and not-thereness
are loosely intermingled

so it comes as a shock when he's gone.
I surface into sunlight.
Thrilled children on the shore
shout 'Woman, show us the seal.'
But the seal is not for showing.

WATERFALL AT HALLANE

Leaps, a dazzle of splinters,
sheer into the rock pool
or cut short at high tide
dibbles showers in the sea.

Spring-fed up the valley,
no drought ever staunched that
crystalline downpour. Its flow
could be old as a stone.

But we saw it immobilise
once, when cold unrecalled
in the annals of weather
carved a tree trunk in ice.

It melted slowly, drip
and drip cleaving fissures
until the ice-bark creaked
to the axe of the sun.

Then the sluicing began.
From the spring on the moor,
from runnel and field drain
foregathering waters

Came slapping and lurching
round rocks, over tree roots,
cattle-ruts, weed beds, nose
down on scent of clean salt.

Late one mild night we heard it,
the roar of full spate,
of deliverance. When the waters broke
we raced out to be in at the birth.

LOW TIDE AT SPRINGS, GOLANT

Slowly, porpoise-shaped, the banks emerge
Shiny and wet, not mud of river margins
But sand, surprising and splendid, gold
Hidden in the river bed for exceptional tides
To discover. And on these lavish strands
The random shoal of bright boats lies impacted.

All the village is there, drawn by the dream-like
Strangeness, the marvellous paradox,
To walk where water was. Delirious dogs
Dare-devil after pebbles,
Small children slippy as fish
Splash in the shallows, dart round dug-in keels,
And drown in rollicking wonder.
Old men with bags and spades,
Never-before-seen doubled-up denizens
Of some weird watery sub-world,
Squelch down river over hump and hollow
To dig for worms, the air of festival
Turning bowed labour to buffoonery.

It is all so brisk and buoyant in the sunlight,
So holiday hilarious, so here and now,
That nothing prepares one for this wistful sense
Of being present at a scene gone by,
Children and dogs and men arrested there,
Sealed in the rounded amber of a day,
Far archetypal figures in a dream
Of impossibly Arcadian summer.

But now the seldom sands recede again,
Curlew and heron come wading to pick over
Fast dwindling strands, and land-logged listing boats
Swan upright. Soon, only Christ could walk there.
The moon, wan woman gaping with fatigue
Ends revelry, sets all to mundane order,
With punctual hands draws up the river's cover.

STONE WILDERNESS

Here at the crusted edge of land
steep shingle crunches to our feet
and razor sharp the small waves clip
the line where flux and fixture meet.

Nothing of comfort here. The banks
of rounded pebbles, white and grey,
are desert structured by a tide
that dragged the loam of life away.

But see, the sage and sturdy find
their means, insinuate their roots
and keep their heads down, grow and thrive
and bear their horned and berried fruits.

Seakale, horned poppy, silverweed,
stealthy poisonous bittersweet,
mauve mallow and bright tormentil
obey the precept, take and eat.

No jostling tangling plant life here.
Lone squatters, each marks out a place.
Who shares the hard and single bed
sees in each flower a fellow face.

BODRUGAN'S LEAP

I'm recalling the legend
of Bodrugan's horse
leaping over this abyss

where we sit gazing
across a sea like glass
that reflects the evening's opal.

'It was young Bodrugan' you say
'who dived into the abyss
frenzied to foil the King's men'.

'Died, of course.' 'What of the horse?'
'Oh, that was the other Bodrugan.'
'A fated name,' I say.

The sea is darkening. Sun down
comes early on this coast of hills.
High tide slaps on the rocks below.

And suddenly I am aware
of the lure, the pull to leap
until you take my hand

and say 'Time to get out of here.'

HERON

His slow flight is a different semaphore
To that of oystercatchers, curlews, gulls,
A message unconcerned and leisurely.
He comes, a solitary, to fish the shore

In small bright sky-reflecting pools,
And stands so hunched, so hands-behind-the-back,
Even his stance has little of a birds'
Quick stillness. Casual, now and then he strolls

Looking, you'd think, for coloured glass or shells,
(Only a human shows such aimlessness).
Till, in a striking moment, he's a spear
That springs to life the instant that he kills.

ENCOUNTER

Making way on the cliff path
'any private place to sleep round here?'
Asked as a joke. A lithe and lively girl
with a keen eye for a chat.
Said she'd walked twelve miles
which, when she told her route
we calculated all of twenty-five.
Tired? Well, ready to pitch the tent.
Came from up North, travelled
on foot and bike, Scotland, Ireland,
now here, God knows, to get away.

Then the unlikely 'see you',
hitch of the pack and gone.
Snap decision. Chasing after her,
(she'd nipped as fast as a stoat)
we said kip down in our garden.
No waver. Quick assent.
We gave her kitchen supper,
bread, cheese, two jugs of cider
which she downed with a desert thirst.
Hungry, and starved for talk
she ate fast, talked fast.
Got it off her chest. Father
intemperate, mother gone to pot.
Schooled by nuns, then joined the Born Agains,
good till you get to know they're hypocrites.
After emotional crisis, unspecified,
Breakdown. A rather cheery Councillor
must have done something, she was still 'down here'.
A sad and usual story. But she clowned it.
Waves of laughter carried us to bed.

I woke twice in the night.
A full moon paved the sea.
Thought of her lonely in her tent.
Scrub that, sleeping soundly.
Heard the tide come in, scrunching on pebbled shore.
Then slept, dreamt her as Visitant,
the nun concerned with educating girls.

She left us after breakfast
waving the card that printed our address.
'I want to send you a line,'
it never came. Like a bird
she'd flown her once-time nest
head-on for a future, Social Services,
well, something meaningful - as it was vague.

There was no trace of her night's encampment.
No dint in the grass. Not so much
as a single burnt-out matchstick.
In fact a perfect guest. Her brief stay
remains like a page in a commonplace book
marked red, Remember This.

THE SNAKE

That lissom creature coils about my mind
like a snagged thought inimical to sleep.
I don't know why he has this power to keep
coming and coming. Well, each day he'd wind
his suave length through long grass, rippling and
S-bending secretly. His ways were deep,
yet he was timid and guileless. Poor creep
to be so branded, with his small head signed
by an arrow, marking him venomous.
He lapped saucers of milk, basked on the stone
of the old well. Lay sleek as a clean cat.
And for about a fortnight stayed with us
quite at his ease. There's no way to atone.
The man meant well. Being man is like that.

CRAFTSMAN

'Shed at end of garden' the notice said.
So we followed the concrete path. It led
Past coal bunker, dustbins, pots of flowers,
Roses, jasmine, big spikey dahlias

To a workshop marked P.J. Treleaven.
A tall white-haired gangling youth of a man
With a clay-pit pallor, he took us in,
Both senses, shook hands, assessed our grain

As customers, or strangers from up-country -
You couldn't tell. But that shrewd cock of the eye
Made us aware that we were here on his terms.
Only fools cross frontiers carrying arms.

I could have mis-read him; so instant the switch
To business. Formica, yes, he had a cache
Of the stuff, big bendy sheets stacked upright.
Three-ply. When he cut and planed it straight

It didn't seem right that no shavings curled
Crisply, that the honest clean smell of wood
Didn't splice the air. Something solid, a hull,
Should grow from those hands, from birth in that skull.

A craftsman. He showed the proper way to fit;
Slats of cardboard placed under the lowered sheet,
Withdrawn when each edge homed true. Simple skill
Imparted simply. One time, he'd have been humble.

But now. Deal accomplished, he showed us his pride
Of cactus dahlias, wild flower patch, well-fed
Beans, marrows. Mentioned his passion for jazz.
A new man, rooted still in chapel-strict ways,
An Elder (we learned) - easily balancing
God's will with his will, and the world's turning
With a strong stance in the old style. He'd made good
The rift between formica and seasoned wood.

SLOW WORMS

The name insults them.
Fangless snake or legless lizard
their chequered sleekness
dry as clean silk to the touch
is pure reptilian.

They bask on our top step
in a smooth coil, but angled
by the neat jut of the head.
Slip through our fingers
like sand, immediately
reconstitute their poise.

Their lowly presence
diminishes each summer.
When holiday-hippy
we live stark in the garden
gone wild through long absence

We miss them, earth creatures,
doomed amongst those who troop
in reverse from the saving Ark.
Their humble use too slight
to spare them the world's clout.

FOR IONE, MY AUNT

I remember Lizzie saying
'She turned back to wave
so I knew it was the last time.
She turned at the corner
there by the grey willow
and smiled, and said goodbye.'

Now when I walk that stony path
I hear with her ears the sea,
mew of a circling buzzard,
curlews whistling clear notes
as they turn to breast the hill,
and I think of that brave farewell.

For when in my childhood we parted
she'd kiss me and say 'don't cry.
Look forward - this isn't an ending.
So long as life lasts remember
that you should never look back'.

POEMS OF ESSEX &
HOME IN STEBBING

THE OLD HOUSE

I count time in centuries. I've clocked up five of them.
I remember taper and candle, the sand and the rushes;
Slats for the fitting of boards still groove my window beams.

A priest's house, I am ample and high ceilinged,
Solidly built, without frivolous decoration.
Though fashion or neglect has modified
My original proud austerity
I have resisted excess.

Now I am host to three chiming clocks
And several periods of furniture.
She who arranges my festal flowers
With careless disregard, placing them
Frivolously, where they can catch the light
is, did she know it, my tenant.

For I have no owners, only transient guests
who talk, make love and sweep me
and are careful of my fabric. Grade 2
Is my classification. I bear the insult,
As the deposed priest who sheltered Edmund Campion
Bore his martyrdom, but I admit, more lightly.

Some day I'll be put on the market.
Whoever thinks he buys me must beware.
I'll put lines on his brow, agues in his joints
And whisper at dawn of his mortality.

POPLAR MUSIC

Hear how it rains. Even on blue clear days
Hear how it rains. Sometimes a shower as light
As flocks of finches rustling into flight
Patters the air, but still the parched grass stays
Brittle as stubble, and a cloudless sky
Winks through bright leaves at our perplexity.

Or else a downpour, with a gusting wind
To lash it slantwise batters on the panes;
But sunlight, flung across the grass in skeins,
Shows this wild rain to be of the same kind
As that soft shower, the leaves unceasing clash
Making of gale a soak, of breeze a splash.

Though in high summer there may come a trance
Of heavy heat-calm, when the leaves lie still,
With only one dark twirler there to spill
Its single drop. Then, in a measured dance,
The seed, the poplar snow, drifts to the ground,
True fall at last, accomplished without sound.

WINTER LANDSCAPE, ESSEX

Snow falls, the present falls away
And earth is innocent again.
Quiet in named beds the holy dead
Lie still beneath one counterpane.

The time has come for miracles.
Water is rendered into ice.
White ferns grow up the window pane.
The surpliced trees are leafed in lace.

That secret birth in Bethlehem
Has come to pass, as children know,
In the wreathed church; and starry eyes
See a bright portent in the snow,

That iron cold will melt away
And earth grow living green again
But somehow still be undefiled.
God grant goodwill unto all men.

SKRITCH HOWLE

'her burial roundel crunketh in howling'
As ghosting the graveyard
Practising witchcraft
On broomstick of breastbone,
Herself cat-familiar, she rode dark
In a light cloak, loaded with presages
Of impendent evils, the long fire
In the long house, the interminable howling.

No longer mystical, she is still
Singular. Face as flat as a plague,
With eyes that reel like wheels,
She makes light of pitch dark.
Falls quiet as snow on small prey,
Wings articulating silence.
Can needle a quick mouse
In thick grass.

She inhabits our willow.
Black ivy enshrines the niche
Where she stands, a pale Madonna,
Bending on me her gaze,
Her blink of absolution.
I hold my breath for fear
Of her fear, whose shadowy retreat
Bodes me no ill, leaves guilt in its wake, unshriven.

CONVERSATIONS

The owl calls twice. First sleepily,
a fluffed tremulous falsetto.
Her second cry rings clear,
tingles the nerve ends of darkness.

Time waits on the space between trees.
Then you hear it, the long-drawn quaver
of owl replying to owl. The note
is perfect attunement. They talk

the same language of echoes;
but such a comfortable repetition.
They may be discussing the whereabouts
of mice, or just locating position.

Here in the house clock answers clock.
The grandfather in the hall strikes
eleven. From the living room
the bracket clock reverberates

quietly two minutes after. Soft talk
enumerating hours. Out of time,
in accord. Let's synchronise
words. They should agree too, roughly.

THE RELIC

I watched as they dug out
a bone from an obsolete
grave; shafted walls
for a newcomer's habitation.

Jocular, they pitched
calcium into long grass.
No sorrowing now.
His funny bone

Will lie with the shards
of old pots, wired wreaths,
the stiff unfading
squalor of plastic flowers.

Well, he had to make way
for a fresh row;
named, bright headstones,
little gardens,

But it seems sad
that he's unearthed
like Pharaoh's gold,
no museum piece

But a fragmented man
who spoke the old tongue,
trod out thin roads
still winding, without reason,

Around lost obstacles.
When I brake at a bend
I sometimes think of him,
alien in long exile

From his worked homeland
which is ours now
to drug as we please
spending his thrifty loam.

SCYTHING

I know these June days by the rasp of stone
on blade, a steady rhythmic scanning
like the thrust and pull of a saw, making
a gritty tuneless reiteration.
Then silence. Geoff is flicking a deft thumb
along the honed edge. You know by his whistle
it's fit, and then that he's standing to sum
up the field, its green surf set for the hiss he'll
draw from a thousand decapitations. Grass
will shatter gracefully before him. Seed heads
powder air with pollen dust. He'll amass
half a haystack in a day, but firstly, laid
in concentric arcs, the perfect swathes will lie
scythe-shaped, signed proof of artistry, to dry.

IN THE CHURCHYARD

A sound so strange; a little like a throng
Of finches on the thistles; something akin
To starlings on a roof, whose lively din
Of whistles, clicks and cooings is no song
But sweeter than most singing. I looked to see
What in the world such sibilance could be.

And saw the children. Twosomes, hand in hand,
Long-coated, small and neat, and at a guess
Orphans or waifs - a sameness in their dress,
A look of being united in a band
Made them seem so - they stepped through the long grass,
Marshalled and lectured by their governess

Who, briskly kind, was showing them the church,
Pointing out buttresses, gargoyles, and gravestones
Tilted and mossed, engraved with skull and bones.
They jostled close as lovebirds on a perch,
Intent with pleasure in their Sunday spree;
A perfectly happy, sad small company.

PLANTING SNOWDROPS

There could have been no better afternoon
For planting snowdrops by the lichened pear;
Over the lawn the dead leaves damply strewn,
Thrushes and robins singing piercing clear
As if their songs were echoing on stone;
Limpid as cool water the pale air,
The trees picked clean by winter to the bone.

I tasted deep the season as I set
The small white waxen bulbs in crumbling loam,
Some wick'd with green, and other ones as yet
Showing no promise of the spring to come.
It seemed so still, the air, the willows traced
Like tributaries black against the sky,
The buttress of the church with ivy chased,
The chink of rutted water like an eye
Blinded and white, yet printed clear as mine
With leaves and clouds. No dulcet summer day
Could be, I thought, so delicate and fine
As this one chiselled from the year's decay.

ANGLE SHADES

'Are seen most months of the year.'
Fly-by-nights, quite common
if you've an eye for seeing
moths in the dark. Still, I wonder

How did this Owlet come
to assemble herself just there
clipped to the frozen pane? Flaunting
her ethnic colours, her mask

Of a warrior, the fiercely
painted eyes blazoned athwart
the rib and lacing of forewings.
This room is a sealed box.

Immigrant flying in
on autumnal winds,
mild missile homing in
on the dangerous lamp

Mysteriously here
I find her sleeping.
It is the winter solstice.
She will wait a long time

For summer's warm enticement
to shaft in the moon-white garden
pale night-flowers that give suck
from honeyed nectaries.

We share this night's cold quiet
in our twin solitudes
silent as snow-fall; waiting
for something remembered.

THE FOX EARTH

I had to keep returning to the place
as if in search of something I had lost,
knowing it wasn't there. Under the gorse
the raw dug earth was like a mouth aghast,
as violence rips the throat. I'd hear the spade's
loud excavation, yelp of terriers,
the digger's shout. That night the woods
Howled with the vixen's pitiful despairs,
her frantic searching. The guilt was mine.
I'd found the earth and stupid with elan
told them, never suspecting what was to be done.
So I returned, all that Spring holiday
to watch, search, listen, knowing it was true,
the silence, and a presence gone away.

ODE TO A BLACKBIRD

My heart lifts when I hear our garden's king,
The Blackbird, perched on roof or budding branch,
Loose from his vibrant throat a paean to Spring
That no dark mood or grief of mine can stanch.
He shouts the song I heard once, long ago,
Ring out above a clanging London street,
An affirmation of the years rebirth
As made the pavements glow,
And fastened wings to my town-wearied feet,
And flew me not aloft, but back to earth.

Spirit and earth are one, his song proclaimed,
And every living thing an aura wears,
A Brightness, something scarcely to be named
But which, in wakened instances, appears
To eyes rinsed clean; it gives a humble weed
The sparkling soul and status of a star,
And shows a dance of midges to be one
With cosmic measures: need
Is all the spirit asks, to be aware
Of heavens, close as warmth of heart, or sun.

CYPRESS

The cypress crowding our roof is deemed unsound.
'Take a risk if you wish, but I'd say clear fell,'
is the experts' advice. It's not so simple
a choice if you love that green ample
presence, known for years. I gaze at it, meanwhile,
to print its configuration on the mind -

A pointless exercise, for trees are not
paintings. Picture them as you will
it's the loud, brisk, seething life in them that
you're going to miss. A high wind at night
soughing through branches like a big sea swell
to rock you asleep, that's what you won't forget.

Then, the eventful birds, goldcrests, warblers
too slippy to be identified as
'garden' or 'willow', packs of longtailed tits
swinging upside down like acrobats,
a once-only night jar - oh yes, it's these
endearing and elusive wanderers

Whose lack will sting. And the tree's bright selfhood,
it's seasonal moods, boisterous in Autumn,
in summer all drowsing peace; that sharp scent
loosed after rain - think of these being absent.
In miniature, here is the human problem;
risk following the heart, or keep the head?

ROUNDABOUT
(A Suffolk name for a tub-shaped pony trap)

At first I thought that I mis-heard
The sound that jerked my heart awake.
It seemed the kind of odd mistake
Sense stumbles on when one is tired.

But soon, hooves clopping up the hill,
The grate of wheels, a lantern's glow,
Told me before it came in view
That whether by my wish or will,

A pony and a roundabout
Were jingling through the summer night,
Whose harness bells had put to flight
Hours of disquietude and doubt.

I never guessed from where they came
Unless they lit from out of time,
Nor why they reason made, and rhyme
Of matters that stayed just the same

But for this fact, that life looked odd,
No longer worn and commonplace,
And showed a brief bewitching face,
And gave a wink and then a nod.

RESCUE OPERATION

Field mouse, bright as a conker,
Just like a bookworm
You have found your cage
to be place for browsing.
In your ivory hands
the metal bars are held
as if they could open
on worlds of exploration.
What do you read
as you gaze out
on our fantastical lives?
Words are gobbledegook
in your shell-pink intelligent ears,
are less decipherable
than concourses of bird song.
A smile does not alarm.
You sniff the air upwards.
Your lambent eyes
are solid round brown tears.
We who saved you from Grimalkin
will soon release you
into the danger of freedom,
glad to see you go,
missing your trust.

COWS

They're
Angular and spikey as if stitched
By a six-year-old whose palaeolithic eye
Sees like a camera; bright hides patched
Like a quilt, irregularly even:
Shapes enriched
By snap illusion of mobility.
Note the hitched
Tail of the stampeder, the raised hoof
Of the inveterate pail kicker
Poised to jump over the moon.
The sampler is grass green,
The cows a pattern, stretched
Frieze-wise over the hatched
Shadows of hedgerow trees.
Twice each day they are fetched
By a primitive shout, and wend
Their slow way over the ley.
Their pace is not of our day.
But when, for once, detached
Enough to stand and be watched
By their tranquil Buddha's eye,
Their all-consuming eye,
Then, briefly, nor are we.

THE FLAT LANDS

We have no mountains
recalling harsh birth pangs.
Earth shock is alien here,
The mood pastoral.

This outstretched land remembers
How sheep shorn turf would march
The unhedged long horizons
And flocks race to a standstill.

It is Cistercian country.
Enter a week-day church,
You meet walled up in there
A homely holiness. The white monks knew

Their spirit's region, apt with drenching springs,
Retentive clay for carp ponds,
Tilted ground where vineyards
Hugged hot flints after sundown.

Still, even now - seismic Combines halted
And slick of burning stubble
Dispersed on the wind's currents, -
There will come a perennial hour

When the land spawns recollections.
Only Sunday bells and blackbirds
Shake a long discarded silence
That falls again, as leaden as a plummet

On distances that repeat themselves
Over and over to the line of sky,
World's end to weaver, monk and shepherd,
Our longing finds new light and plenty there.

HAIKU

The wasp jar is full.
Who will eat the fallen plums?
Two sweets, but one choice

******

Eve in the garden
Forbidden one fruit. Did God
Know woman so well?

******

Night pumps this old house
with silence. Three quiet clocks tick.
The fourth, whose loud heart?

******

Clocks count each second,
at midnight strike off a day.
But time keeps no time.

******

Blooms, the Xmas rose
Too late for its festival.
How early, the spring!